TAKE FIVE 04

TAKE FIVE 04

SHANTA ACHARYA

CLARE CROSSMAN

JOHN GOHORRY

CHRISTOPHER PILLING

JOHN WESTON

Shoestring Press

All rights reserved. No part of this work covered by the copyright hereon may be reproduced or used in any form by any means – graphic, electronic, or mechanical, including copying, recording, taping, or information storage and retrieval systems – without written permission of the publisher.

Typeset and printed by Q3 Print Project Management Ltd,
Loughborough, Leicestershire.
(01509) 213456

Published by Shoestring Press
19 Devonshire Avenue, Beeston, Nottingham, NG9 1BS
(0115) 925 1827
www.shoestringpress.co.uk

First published 2004
© Copyright: Shanta Acharya, Clare Crossman, John Gohorry, Christopher Pilling and John Weston
The moral right of the author has been asserted.
ISBN: 1 904886 09 4

Shoestring Press gratefully acknowledges financial assistance from
Arts Council England

Contents

SHANTA ACHARYA

Highgate Cemetery	3
Memories	4
Farewell Ghazal	5
Silent Witness	6
Coconut Milk	7
Missing	8
A Kind of Going Home	9
Remembering With Flowers	10
Remembering Gandhi	11
Bori Notesz	12
Mental Chemistry	14
Loneliness	15
It Was Your Voice	16
Homecoming	17
Losing, Finding	18
I Do Not Know	19

CLARE CROSSMAN

I. The Shell Notebook Poems	23
Migrations	23
James Morrow	24
Sailing from France: Henrietta's Romance in 1698	25
Quilt	26
Land of the Rain	27
Talamh an Eisc (Kitty's song)	28
Henrietta's Great-Granddaughter Considers (1798)	29
Sleep Music	30
Lament for Philip Cox	31
II. Lantern Slides	32
Dundalk Daguerrotype, 1862	33
Portrait of Janetta in 1902	34
The Ballad of the Callieach	35
Mona Writes of Troubles (1912)	37
Postmarked 1924	38
Lantern Slides	39

JOHN GOHORRY
Eight Chinese Verses
1. 43
2. 44
3. 45
4. 46
5. 47
6. 48
7. 49
8. 50

CHRISTOPHER PILLING
Midwinter Life Class 53
Midsummer Life Class 61

JOHN WESTON
The Launch 72
Winchmore Hill 1944 73
My Father 74
Out of the Blue 75
Scillies in April 77
Edwardes Square 78
Last Rites 80
To Alaska and Back 82
A Fair Thought 83
House, at Denbigh Gardens 84
Giving Way 85
Talisman 86
Above Normal 87
Grandparents 89
To Our First Grandchild, Day One 90
Sighting 91
Moving with THE TIMES 92
Fifty Years On 94

Shanta Acharya

was born and educated in India. In 1979, she won a scholarship to Oxford where she completed her doctoral study. Between 1983-5 she was a Visiting Scholar at Harvard. In 1985, she joined Morgan Stanley, an American investment bank, where she trained in asset management in London. She subsequently worked as a portfolio manager for several firms, including Baring Asset Management. She is currently Associate Director, Initiative on Foundation and Endowment Asset Management at London Business School. Her doctoral dissertation, *The Influence of Indian Thought on Ralph Waldo Emerson*, was published in 2001. She has also published two collections, *Numbering Our Days' Illusions* (1995) and *Not This, Not That* (1994). For further information, visit her website: www.shantaacharya.com

Acknowledgment is due to the editors of the following publications in which several of these poems appeared, sometimes in earlier versions:

Ambit, Acumen, Coffee House Poetry, Connections: The Literary Scene In The South, Fire, Iota Poetry Quarterly, New Hope International, Other Poetry, Poetry Nottingham International, The Frogmore Papers, The Swansea Review and *World Literature Written In English* in the UK.

Seeing The Wood And The Trees (Cairde na Coille) in Ireland.

Indian Literature, Kavya Bharati, Poetry Chain, Journal of Literature & Aesthetics and *Samyukta: A Journal of Women's Studies* in India.

HIGHGATE CEMETERY

I wandered among the dead in a cemetery town
exploring the winding paths where angels, carved in stone,
stood silently directing me through the green alleyways.

This island with overhanging yew and trailing clematis,
with unifying ivy nurturing insects, larvae, butterflies and birds
has more to do with the living than the memory of the departed.
We need the solace of the Comfort Corner more than the dead.

Through the hawthorn and blackthorn, field maple and elm
a cool wind blows steadily through our realm.
The voices of children from the playground across the school
confirm the inscription on Karl Marx's tomb:
The philosophers have only interpreted the world
in various ways. The point however is to change it.

Everyday our little world changes a little bit,
whether we like it or not is quite irrelevant.
I imagine a dialogue between Marx and Krishna.
It is easier I confess to alter myself than the world!

When our friends start to leave, it is time
to take stock of our coming and going:
Of those immortal dead who live again
in minds made better by their presence.

In the unmapped terrain within us we bury
in terraced catacombs painful memories.
If only we could let them grow out of us like trees.

MEMORIES

After great pain, a formal feeling comes –
                    Emily Dickinson

The more I try to forget the more I remember.

From now on I will accept ceremoniously
whatever thoughts come unbidden to me even in my sleep,
feelings that burst through the mists of my nervous forgetting,
memories of you that moisten my startled eyes as life's gifts.

When I listen to your CDs of Mozart, I will let the music
fill the infinite between our two souls. I will not try to measure
the extent of my loss in human terms. What good is there
in speculating about what-might-have-been?

I will not build a Pyramid or a Taj Mahal to our friendship
nor will I let the echoes of your words trapped in my limbs
haunt me like ghosts entombed in more formal relationships.
I will let the winds of change scatter my pain like ashes.

I will not change the locks to my heart, body or soul,
nor will I wait for your letter or phone-call.
I will be patient like a stone and let Time be my counsellor.
Perhaps, the less I try to forget the less I will remember.

FAREWELL GHAZAL

When I lie bereft, broken and dejected,
crossed by life, by the wide world rejected,

I rejoice you no longer have to face humiliation –
such is the fate of the human condition.

When darkness descends upon me, thick as fog
obliterating my view, turning my mind into bog

I rejoice you no longer have to endure perdition –
such is the fate of the human condition.

When the slings and arrows of fortune pin me down,
leaving me to lick my wounds, blood trickling from my crown,

I rejoice you no longer have to wrestle with salvation –
such is the fate of the human condition.

When family and friends misunderstand me, and each other,
grief makes children of us all, we cry and fight together,

I rejoice you no longer have to witness alienation –
such is the fate of the human condition.

When death can come in the stillness of the night,
take someone you love and you cannot even put up a fight,

I rejoice you no longer are defined by our limitation –
such is the fate of the human condition.

SILENT WITNESS

'*Dad!*' ... her words rumble forth,
slow thunder after lightening,
the closing of doors, engines hissing,
movement of steel on steel, muffled
her litany of complaints in the Underground.

They pool their luggage on the platform,
he sits beside me on the empty wooden bench,
she hurries off to configure how to reach Angel.
I overhear her checking with a fellow traveller.

It is difficult to tell whether he is hurt,
used to this sort of thing or simply a pain in the butt.
He sits quietly dignified, not displaying any emotion.

When the Bank train finally arrives,
we all get in together, he continues to sit next to me
    and she continues to sit far away from him –
perfect strangers. Other commuters who join us
at Archway, Tufnell Park, Kentish Town, Camden Town
would never have guessed they were related,
thick as blood, father and daughter.

I wanted to tell her as we hurtled along
how fickle death could be at his age,
lurking at every corner, how time is short –
there isn't enough to squander on
    pride or self-absorption;

How sometimes there is not a chance to whisper
Fare well, fare forward Father –

hold his hand, in silent witness and prayer,
touch his feet in reverence, kiss his forehead
or do anything at all; not out of choice
but as when one is drowning, powerless
against the swirling vortex of fate,
forced to face a lifetime without a father.

COCONUT MILK

My basket was heavy with shopping –
mushrooms, peppers, tomatoes, onions,
greens, garlic, ginger, coriander leaves,
cottage cheese, chick peas, prawns –
only the coconut milk was missing.

My local Sainsbury did not have the ready-to-cook
variety, comes in a tin, made in Thailand –
white and creamy as full-fat milk and just as silky.

Will this do? The kind-looking, withered shop assistant
enquired, handing me a solid cake of coconut milk.
I nodded, smiled; he smiled, shuffled off, satisfied.

Later that evening when I cook the prawns
with finely chopped onions, mushrooms, tomatoes
and garlic, gently adding the grated coconut milk,
stirring, the flavours blending, simmering,
wafting through the wide-open window into the world
moving to the rhythm of old Hindi film songs
    we enjoyed listening together –
I am filled with your presence beside me:

Gazing at the resplendent sun, ready to retire
behind the trees, responding
    to the *raga* and *rasa* of living –
the playing, crying, working, dreaming, loving –
urging me to see that like the sun, moon and stars
you are always there though briefly revealed to us;
here our paths diverge and I must let go...

Sprinkling the freshly chopped coriander leaves,
the ground garlic and crushed chilli on the curry,
my eyes are blinded with grief and a child's fury.

MISSING

It is that feeling on first awakening
at dawn to the matins of bird song,
your face playing hide-and-seek as the sun
peers through the mists among the trees –
my body moving into the light
    slowly filling with meaning.

I whisper your name like a mantra
as if the mere repeating of your name
can restore you to me. Even in my sleep,
I know you are no longer here –
not just an absence in our family photographs.

A tree immersed in snowy forgetfulness,
I am cursed to loose my flowers and leaves –
dreaming of buds, newly sprung leaves and a festival
of flowers to rescue me from this bareness of being.

I dream of you and mother on the white steed of spring,
having waited patiently all these years for my leafing.
I stand alone, your daughter, without offspring –
reaching for the foot of the rainbow crying…

I discern your features in every stranger's face, lips
as they transform into a smile in our nondescript streets.

When the sun sets and the stars begin their vespers,
I recognise the myriad ways of our losing and finding.

A KIND OF GOING HOME

For one precious, unforgettable day
you were loaned to us, only to be taken away.
I knew you not but like a shaft of light
you penetrated my inner emptiness
making me look unsparingly upon your death
    as a kind of going home.

After months of preparing for your homecoming,
for the safe, though premature, arrival
of their dreams sublimated in your fragile body;
    your parents never for one instant
admitting any impediment in welcoming you
    home as the heart of their family.

In the beginning, when you kicked and frolicked
    exploring the limits of your navigations
inside the high seas of your mother's womb,
we monitored your progress introducing ourselves
as you levitated saintlike in your space capsule.

Considering how everything
    that could go wrong, did go wrong,
your clear rejection of our world makes perfect sense.
You left a mother shorn of her dreams, bereft of hope,
and a father confounded, not knowing how to cope
with the permanent nature of your departure,
knowing of no fit ceremony to reconcile dreams with reality.

Your brief sojourn unleashed a groundswell of emotions
darkening earth and sky into one granite ocean of confusion
    after your exit banished rationality out of fashion.

I do not know what you looked like when they set their
eyes upon you struggling for your life in an incubator.
    I can only see their faces, cadaverous masks –
of your father, my brother; your mother, my sister-in-law –
frozen in incandescent grief, their expressions raw
like a Francis Bacon painting, horror contained,
depicting tragedy overwhelming for any philosophy.

REMEMBERING WITH FLOWERS

The bunch of bluebells on your windowsill
are for constancy; there's honeysuckle
for devotion and affection. I invest meaning in flowers
as I wait for a sign from you in the retreating light.

I brought you field flowers to remind you of past times –
buttercups, cowslips, dandelions and wild violets.
I have come with a potted jasmine for our friendship.

Do you remember how we wove garlands for our pujas,
with marigolds, hibiscus, bougainvillea, kenna, lilies –
flowers that were given by our neighbours to get rid of us
in the tree climbing, limb bruising days of our adolescence?

We took leaves of grass to decorate our handiwork,
left huge brass pots of palm trees to mark the *mandap*.
We painted the earth by night with rice paste;
you were best with Lakshmi's feet, I did the rest.

You told me secret tales under the orange blossom,
I believed in all your magical words as we planted
bashful peonies, dainty daisies and virginal lupins in the garden,
watered the sunflowers that never tired of gazing at the sun.
Roses were incorruptible in your hands even as they blushed.

I could have worn a bleeding poppy, but I speak with its
shattered heart though you cannot hear me. If I do your puja
with daffodils, lilies and iris, tendrils of blue clematis,
decorate your garland with deep green holly and ivy,
will you at least open your eyes and speak to me?

REMEMBERING GANDHI

Turning the other cheek, you got the upper hand;
with Swadeshi and Satyagraha, coined your brand.

Ace architect of freedom, the deconstruction of a nation
transformed you into a saint, to some a shrewd politician.

You marched all over India to touch the Untouchable,
called them the Children of God, and declared Home Rule.

Your fasts unto death plunged your peers into confusion,
transformed you into a saint, to some a shrewd politician.

You trusted women, included them in your entourage;
your charisma, half-naked fakir, upset the Raj.

Your experiment with truth, sex and religion,
transformed you into a saint, to some a shrewd politician.

The Viceregal Palace was haunted by your steel-rimmed spectacles,
bald head, loin-cloth, wiry body, walking stick and chappals.

Your towering above Nehru, Jinnah and Mountbatten,
transformed you into a saint, to some a shrewd politician.

What price, in perpetuity, we pay for the partition of our homeland,
the splintering of a subcontinent, giving birth to a wasteland?

Nobody understood you, Mahatma; Bapu of the nation
transformed into a saint, to some a shrewd politician.

In the end, it was a Hindu fanatic reaching for your feet,
lodged a bullet in your heart as you breathed your last.

Your life, a journey of self-discovery overcoming illusion,
transformed you into a saint, to some a shrewd politician.

BORI NOTESZ *

(for *Miklós Radnóti*)

If I placed my faith in miracles
    thinking there was an angel walking beside me,
do not judge me for my thoughts were only of you –
    I cannot die, and cannot live, without you.
I saw the blue of your eyes in the sky
    shining like the angel's sword protecting me
as I fell, a ghost in the glow of dawn.
But I was lifted by invisible wings
    and marched on ignoring the ditch's embrace.

As long as I knew my way back to you,
    I was prepared to walk on live coals,
bear witness to the barbarism of human beings
    for man is the lowest of all the animals –
setting houses, fields and factories on fire,
    streets overrun with burning people, men twisted,
then like a snapped string they sprang up again, dead;
    twitching like a broken twig in the ditch.
Women screamed as children were dashed
    against walls: *What is the purpose of this, Lord?*
I asked. I survived, fixing my thoughts on you.
You were the constant in this churning, smoking mess.

I can only leave you my anger, my powerlessness
    at finding my world in ruins, left with neither
faith nor hope, compassion nor redemption;
    for I know nothing can save me now...

If I placed my faith in miracles
    thinking that there was an angel walking beside me,
judge me only by my thoughts of you in a world rebuilt
    where my song will live and be heard...
I cannot die, and cannot live, without this thought.

* In November 1944, near the Hungarian town of Abda, Radnoti was shot, along with twenty-one other crippled and emaciated captives, while being forced-marched towards Germany during the liberation of the Balkans. His body was exhumed from a ditch after the war, and identified from the notebook (*Bori Notesz*) of poems in his raincoat pocket. I am indebted to various translations of *Camp Notebook* in the writing of this poem, in capturing his 'voice' as reflected in the Notebook.

MENTAL CHEMISTRY

(For *Kate Barton*)

'Caught midway between was and must be'
    Kate Barton

She pours her vitality on the canvas
dispersing, veiling, transforming her creations;
a process of painting purely alchemical
exploring the volatile nature of her world.

The defined field, the warm pond, where float
groups of cell-like clusters, radiating from single,
multiple nodes; lighter, sometimes darker in hue:

In a luminous plasma of blue-grey sky, red-earth sea,
unfathomable, ethereal black holes humming
secret harmonies, music of destruction, creation –
capturing her body's battle with cancer.

When multicellularity goes wrong
it does not lead to the dawn of a new intelligence,
only a growing eclipse wiping out the universe.

Random yet controlled the interaction of turpentine
and varnish on oil-paint emitting dynamism;
though impermanence and instability are never far behind:

Nature Matter, Earth Matter, Chemical Matter,
Urban Matter, Deconstructed Matter –
matter always turning into spirit, the Other.
Something suspended, held over, still to come.

All her *Untitled* paintings are directions
to fare forward in a time of uncertainty:
The Cultural Sciences – pink, red, blue, green –
each cell purposeful, logical, sublime...

LONELINESS

Sore red, splayed silently in pain, the dappled sky,
a woman bleeding, giving birth, dying,
sacrificing her body in the cycle of creation.
Loneliness is a mother holding her son crucified.

It is that lying awake at 4am feeling,
anaesthetized by the faces of dead children.
Iphigenia, Irma, Alice, Shanti, Xian...
The names and faces scroll on from all over the world.
Loneliness is coming home to an empty pram filled with toys.
Loneliness is when your young wife dies in childbirth.

Loneliness stalks everywhere, like air;
even in the core of deepest love, it is there.
Loneliness has been experienced at the height of ecstasy.
It is our saviour, so make friends with loneliness.

It is the human condition, a vocation;
passed on from generation to generation.
In it you can experience the road not taken,
or the loneliness of a musical instrument untouched,
not breathed into, not played by passionate human
hands. Loneliness is banished, temporarily,
when two people come together in love.
Loneliness is when you have no one to love.

Discover in loneliness the continents of your self;
it is a secure place to wander in for nobody can trespass
unless you let them in. It is an island of freedom and peace.

IT WAS YOUR VOICE

(For *Lily Baden-Powell*)

It was your voice on the answering machine
that eclipsed my world. Yet knowing
you could not return my call, I waited all evening.

It was as if you were on holiday,
a long journey from which you would undoubtedly
return to those you love so dearly.
What is it like being there, dear Lily?

I cannot mourn you properly as I never saw you die;
even a funeral service will fail to convince me.
Death had been kind leaving me
with other crosses to bear, other tears to dry.

When they said you were in hospital,
I remembered the conversation we had.
I was almost there, a raging fever in me;
with your flowers and phone calls steadying me.

News came that you had gone into a coma,
yet we remained unfrozen among the living.
This gravitational force of life,
feeling the pleasure of our physical being.

The voices of your children kept expertly chiselling
away at the silent image of Harry's missing.
Sharing sunsets with my parents in the Lake District,
I learnt how the soul reconciles itself to its fate.

Untimely was the call for your body to stop breathing,
this unloading of soul from carcass;
our unpreparedness for this ritual separation.

HOMECOMING

In every city I visit, in every cathedral or mosque,
pagoda or temple, gurudwara or synagogue;
in every space *enroute* to a kind of self discovery,
I light a candle, offer a prayer.

With every prayer, I wish for things –
some material, others not so tangible, for myself
or for others I have loved more than you.

All through the hours of my worship, I converse with you
about my family and friends, whom you have gifted to me.
I don't know why I presume you will listen more carefully to
my entreaties in a foreign land. I am the one on holiday, not you.

I share my thoughts with you hoping that in the end
you will talk to me, directly; not through your silence.
I imagine you love me because sometimes,
    quite unexpectedly –
you respond to the smallest desire of mine.

How can I forget it was you
who taught me to accept my need of you?
I try to recall our state of bliss before I was born,
before I demanded my own life, separate from you.

If you got hurt, you never showed me.
Instead you loved me unfailingly,
kept watch over me as I lived and got hurt.
How was I to know the consequences of my deeds?

My loneliness has brought me back to where I had begun.
I have nowhere else to go; don't turn me away again on
another journey of self discovery for I am done.

LOSING, FINDING

During a lifetime we lose to gain legacies
   dear as innocence, childhood, youth,
health, wealth, faith, love, freedom,
   one's country and culture.
Even the knowledge of what parents,
   grandparents, siblings, friends,
lovers and enemies mean to us
   is purchased at inexorable cost.

By the time we are able to take stock
   of a lifetime of losses, draw up
an inventory of our inheritance
   before venturing forth to another world –
Life plays its inimitable part in compensating us
   with each asset stripped off from our heart.

To know the true worth of our endowment
   we must lose it first, unexpectedly,
perhaps through some benign personal neglect
   to release the rich flavours from the experience,
without any hope of recompense –
   else knowledge and time make loss-adjusters
of us all, we discount the past, present and future.

I DO NOT KNOW

(After *Shaikh Fakhruddin Ebrahim Hammedani*)

Are you the universe and all existence,
    in all things and beyond all things?
I do not know....

Are you the breath that keeps me alive
    or the moments that take my breath away?
I do not know...

Are you the slayer or the slain, both or neither
I do not know....

Why does your omnipotence tolerate
    so much injustice in this world?
I do not know...

Are you immanent or transcendent,
    unknowable or the One reaching out to us?
I do not know

Do you pour suffering on us
    to mould us towards your purpose?
I do not know....

When I find doubt reigning supreme in my heart,
    is that also your way?
I do not know....

Why do you hide from your creation?
I do not know....

I thought I had an understanding with you
    but you took it away years ago.

Did you replace it with a superior covenant
 or simply reneged on our contract?
I do not know…

If I cannot find you in my heart,
 in the sunset, in the eyes of strangers;
where can I go looking for you,
 let me know for I am tired and bewildered.
I do not know…

If I cannot see your terrible beauty, recognise
 your magnificence, what hope is there for me?
I do not know…

You taught me to find nothing in my heart
 except the compassion of your Love
And yet I do not know…

When will I be released from this separation;
 where do I end, and you begin?
I do not know…

Clare Crossman

Clare Crossman was born in Dartford in Kent in 1954. In 1996 she won the Redbeck competition with her collection *Landscapes*. Since then she has published a sequence of poems *Silent Reading* with Pharos Press to accompany an exhibition of that name. Her last collection of poems entitled *Going Back* was published with Firewater Press in Cambridge in 2003.

The Shell Notebook Poems were started when she was given a Hawthornden Fellowship in 1999. She works in adult education and schools.

Henrietta Baumier was of Huguenot descent. Her forebears when under attack escaped in a little rowing boat down a river running at the back of their home. She married James Morrow of Carnalbana. He was of Scottish descent.

Their daughter Janetta married John Cox of Dundalk in 1895. His father formerly lived on a farm in the Kilmore Township Armagh before settling in Dundalk in 1855. John Cox was one of three brothers, the eldest being Phillip. He and Janetta had two daughters Mona and Norma Cox:

From a fragment found in family papers.

For the god who invented roads and paths.
(Gaelic Inscription found in Yorkshire).

THE SHELL NOTEBOOK POEMS

1. Migrations

At first, an image of two people
pushing off from the firth in a boat,
to a thin line of coast in the distance.
After negotiating the islands,
others from the old farm are there
to meet them, speaking in a tougher tongue.

They disappear, in unknown circumstance.
Return on the Dublin wharves, where they
trade seed and rope with merchants
on the other side of the ocean.
Earth opens on to, walls painted yellow,
a greyhound asleep by the door of a villa,
a room with a piano on which to play music:

photographs brown in the corridors:
men in slouch hats, hold horses.
Girls in lace, push bouquets to the light.
What they had they kept, a shawl,
and a tobacco tin. An echo of ocean
in an upturned shell. They stare out at me.
Their faces their only map.
I catch a glimpse of them, in other streets,
on the Belfast dock where the sky remembers.

2. James Morrow

We followed. After the
harvest failed. Crossing
from the coast of Ayr,

bellows and hammers
in a leather bag. Tongs
for crafting metal.

A maker of wheels I am.
Now turning with them –
slapped with sea-salt in the prow.

Into Ard Macha.

(*I bhfad o bhaile*):
Far from home.
Where rain sweeps in rushes.

(*Taim ag foghlaim na Gaelige*)
Sailing to Ireland.
A bird-man setting down on the shore.

The Englishman comes to make
sure of the rent.
Lights move long after dark.

I observe my face in the lake,
catch fish from its mirror,
learn the darkness of water.

Below Slieve Gullion
the stars have names
in another language.

3. Sailing from France: Henrietta's Romance in 1698

A Spanish sailor told us
it would be safer
to travel at night.
He wore gold earrings that
glimmered like the moon.

We closed the house:
two pairs of shoes,
a coat, a dress.
The oars swept the black river
and we waited for the land to change.

We were pinpricks in the night,
and the heavens were written
upside down, on water.
We were fireflies,
the guttering of a midnight candle.

In the dawn,
we crossed to England.
All day the sea heaved,
around the ship, freighted with
rolls of silk, beneath a linen sail.

I woke, my hair threaded
with laments. My mother's voice
explaining: 'We have nothing but
our silence,
no home, no grace.'

I came back from the fathoms.
On the quay, they took our names.
Years later. I think, I saw the sailor again.
A backward glance.
His hand holding mine, on the shore
of Lough Neagh.

4. **Quilt**

Patchwork of my life here,
emblems of my mother.
Old shirts, a threadbare dress,
cut and sewn together.

Cornflower and poppies
are growing, as they should.
Criss-crossed with plain stitch
like perfectly carved furrows.

I have embroidered our initials
at one corner. Lined it with
linen made of flax. (Blue
midsummer colour).

It's a page of memory.
Square like the turf he cuts.
Hearts and birds,
our names written in scattered ash,

sewn in this silk writing.
Like a book of stories, that falls
on the floor before sleep,
here are fragments shaped.

Our only history, plaited from
the green stems soaked in
brown pond, water
woven to this rough quilt.

Where we can meet,
and are not beaten by
the weather.

5. Land of the Rain

I am a farmer who looks skyward.
I am the keeper of a careful ledger.
I am one of winters' children, when
last grains roll in the bottom of a bin.

I am a servant of the beauty that is snatched.
I am tenant in this mountain clan.
I am whisky, tinker, and a sail.
I am a keeper of a wake for dreams.

I am planted, behind my back.
I am a believer in legend.
I am a stare, in the face
of somewhere ancient.

I am Northern, plaid, rope and cigarettes.
My slate grey house, and hawthorn tree.
I am becoming part of the seeping green,
Fields traced on my mind, as I look up at the stars.

6. **Talamh an Eisc**★
(Kitty's song)

We danced all that night,
to reels and jigs,
under the moon,
a silver bodhran.

The fiddler was drunk,
but his hands stayed steady
as he played the dances
that belong to us all.

Every slow song I was
in Donal's arms.
I felt his warm breath,
his head touching mine.

(He is a native of the long tide,
sailing west on the fleets
to where the catch is plentiful.)

In his eyes I see,
a red headed girl,
and a country inside us
no one can take.

I wear a claddah ringed with
salt from the sea here,
clasped like our hands
as we float across the floor.

Raise a glass to us now and
the ocean we'll be crossing
under tin stars
beaten out from the sky.

Winterman, winterwoman,
gone on the trade routes,
to the Land of the Fish.
(Newfoundland, far North,
where the catch is plentiful.)

★Land of the Fish.

7. Henrietta's Great-Granddaughter Considers (1798)

They only come in summer to the
shuttered house.
The townland children
say lights dance there all year.
They run through the apple orchard,
trying to catch the blossom.
If anyone were living there
they would look down
and see me chasing them home.
I imagine dances, curtsey and gavotte
as I dust the frames of the engravings,
and open darkened rooms.
We hear carriage wheels at 3 a.m.,
horses whipped over the ruts,
shouts as a trunk falls.
Torches blaze,
there's a clank of opening windows.
They make a strange music, the visitors,
like the piano,
and the harp she's always playing.

Below us in the churchyard
someone has tied green ribbons
to hang and rustle from the railings,
and a white owl sits in the graveyard trees.

8. Sleep Music

From the house with the blue door,
there is always music, stories flicker
of places where the woodkerne lived.
Cloaks held by golden clasps,
throwing handfuls of jumping salmon
into a bucket pierced by a pointed stick.

In the house with the blue door,
we doze amongst voices, in the
summer dark. Outside the window,
harvest ripening in the fields.
Wake from that sleep, wind howling
down from the mountain.

In the house with the blue door,
they talk philosophy, threading the night
with conversation, and the old songs.
We go home in the early morning
reply with candles and storm lamp,
thanking for their company:

'Queen of Peace, Pray for us.
May every tribe be blessed'

Lament for Philip Cox

He would have been forty-five now.
Walking out under the wide sky,
greyhound at his heels,

brown hair, blue eyes,
a tall lath of a boy,
going with his father

to catch fish in summer.
His favourite food potato farl,
his music the uilleanns' tune.

He froze one night
didn't wake to rake
the hearth in the morning.

I put pennies on his eyes.
Followed the coffin to the icy peat
for him to sleep with chieftains.

The grounds' wildness his,
we filled the day with stories,
remembering, and left the black fields.

I'll never meet her now,
the one he would have married or
see his handsome face again in children.

He would have been amazed
to see us, as she came home
in the dusk:

making a wake for an old hope,
taking six days to go south,
like five crows on a cart.

II. LANTERN SLIDES

A ship I am under cargo, under sail, with no haven before me
A book I am written in a language from the sky.

From Im Long Measail. Donal O Liathain 1978

1. Dundalk Daguerrotype, 1862

I run through the Monday Streets,
take parcels to the station,
dodge along the quay.
In the dusty office:
I collect names:
'Clover seeds all kinds,
Turnips and swedes'
Letters come in Italian.
I take them to the merchant
he translates them.
He gives me coffee in a steaming cup.
I watch the steamers coming back
loaded with soap and tea,
taking our cargo out
to grow in other fields.
There's a world in wooden boxes.
I can scent
the English apple orchards,
and to the west the salt scales of Maine.
I'm seventeen and want to stowaway,
but we came down through
the gap of the North to a softer country.
I coil ropes wrap them in newspaper
and get sixpence for
every seed I sieve.
On Clanbrassil Street.

2. Portrait of Janetta in 1902

I keep my own counsel in this
house he's built me.
Like my father's in Dunmurry,
a red brick design and pattern.

I like to flow between the rooms,
arrange things as I please.
The row of porcelain figures,
the floral ironstone plates.

I paint in summer.
Collect roses heads for pressing,
I pile my hair high, like other wives,
who go to Dublin for their photograph.

Mr Abernethy puts me beside an aspidistra,
in my best lace blouse and pearls.
Sun sculpture he calls it and
I smile. Afterwards,

I take the girls to coffee.
Norma Constance, Mona Joy,
Ten years between them,
they are always with me.

I lost my two boys in childhood.
Both died at three.
The garden keeps us at
a distance from the street.

A studio portrait is the latest fashion.

3. The Ballad of the Callieach★
(for Norma)

At tea with Suzie on the still blue lake,
he asked me to walk out with him.
His eyes are brown his words are kind,
and he is tall and thin.

O, I would borrow a string of pearls,
let a veil surround my face,
wear a pair of silver shoes
and a dress of Lisburn lace.

With him I can be myself,
not awkward in my buttoned sleeves.
He has given me a locket
I have made him a plait of the last sheaves.

O, I would borrow a string of pearls,
Let a veil surround my face,
Wear a pair of silver shoes
And a dress of Lisburn Lace.

He has given me a hat with feathers.
He has promised me a house in town.
He has given me an emerald ring.
And a bolt of muslin for a linen gown.

O, I would borrow a string of pearls
let a veil surround my face
wear a pair of silver shoes
and a dress of Lisburn lace.

I was called to my father's study,
both of them sitting sternly there,
'We forbid you to see him any more,
and to marry you must not dare'

★Callieach. Traditional plait of corn made at the end of harvest.

On St Stephens Green, one day,
we met in an autumn wind,
I told him it was impossible
that he was not my kind.

O I would borrow a string of pearls
let a veil surround my face
wear a silver pair of shoes
and a dress of Lisburn lace.

At home in the parlour by the paraffin lamp
I imagine I sit with him.
The man who courted me night and day
my dashing, English Captain.

O I would borrow a string of pearls
let a veil surround my face,
wear a silver pair of shoes
and a dress of Lisburn lace.

The season's changed and it's springtime.
There are snowdrops in the lane.
I know that for me now,
life will never be the same.

O, I once borrowed a string of pearls,
dreamed a veil to surround my face,
wore a silver pair of shoes,
was beguiled by Lisburn lace.

4. **Mona Writes of Troubles (1922)**

I call this the House of Superstition.
The maids whisper to each other,
and outside the gates there are
barefoot children.

My mother has turned the peacock feathers to the wall
against bad luck.
Do sailors truly drown when a glass rings?
If I spill salt I must throw it
over my left shoulder.

At night, there are fires.
Once there were soldiers
in the garden, we slept under the bed.
In the morning a bullet hole,
and a pile of shattered glass
on the carpet.
We cannot know them,
so ordinary in suits.
The doctor or the butcher
who meet at midnight in
the surrounding barns.

I push pennies under the gate.
We live on an island in this house.
My father says, this is no longer
an argument over plain scripture.

Outside the window,
lorries prowl the street,
like dinosaurs.

5. **Postmarked 1924**

They walk towards me,
one of the dust of wharves
across the bridges. The woman who
takes barges down the Liffey,
the man in brown tweed
who sells tobacco from a tray.

I have always known them,
the people of this city.
After the ambushes and
the burnings, they spin their
own shapes. Flickering figures,
walking silently, in the damp morning.

I keep company with poets and
painters. In bars and attics,
we discuss how black lines on a bowl
can echo the shape of grass.
the elegance of one circle
at the edge of a cup.

In the Long Room at Trinity,
I found an illustration of the Tea Garden
at Huxinty with a Tower for
Beholding the Moon.
Beyond the cobbles and the colonnades,
there are bright colours:
blue, red, and yellow.

I have pinned the seed pearl butterfly
my mother gave me,
to my coat. There is a country
inside me, and I can sail there,
begin to name it.

6. **Lantern Slides**

Instead of writing letters,
I've brought back, a birthday book,
(small shells hand painted on the cover),
and copies of townland maps.
Crossing to the old country, in the
wake of ocean liners.

(Derek and Sandra. On the steps of
the house where he was born.
4 miles from the border, moss on the
grey stone sills and path. Ivy covering
the windows, and two brown horses
in the barn.)

In my hotel in Belfast, there's a print
of tinkers on the wall. The bar
full of soldiers on weekend leave.
Here sepia is the color of distance and
forgetting. The brown dust from
rubble and graffiti.

Places that are of us come back to us:
in the night I can hear them talking,
in a lighted room downstairs:
Mona, Norma, John
Their reflections at the mirror's edge,
their footfalls certain in my memory.

At Tangradee I stand in the field
where the farm is buried and say outloud
their names.
(Janetta going through the Belfast Streets
to buy ribbons just before she married,
Norma crossing to London, on another salt road).

John Gohorry and Jone Delahaye "Eight Chinese Verses"

John Gohorry has two collections published by Peterloo Poets (1985 and 1992) and his *Life of Merlin* was published by Bullnettle Press, San Francisco, in 1999. His most recent work, *Imagining Dr Minor*, with illustrations by Jone Delahaye, was published by Shoestring Press in 2001.

The artist Jone Delahaye was trained at Somerset College of Art and The Bristol Old Vic Theatre School. A scenic artist, she has had solo exhibitions in galleries in London and the South West.

The form of the *Eight Chinese Verses* was taken from Story 88 in *101 Zen Stories*, transcribed by Nyogen Senzaki and Paul Reps in the latter's *Zen Flesh, Zen Bones* (Arkana, 1991). The relevant passage runs

"A well known Japanese poet was asked how to compose a Chinese poem. 'The usual Chinese poem is in four lines,' he explained. 'The first line contains the initial phrase; the second line, the continuation of that phrase; the third line turns from this subject and begins a new one; and the fourth line brings the first three lines together.'"

Successive third lines in this sequence are intended to reflect the eight stages of zen archery (*kyudo*) described in Kenneth Kushner's book *One Arrow, One Life* (Arkana 1988).

1

In the Street of Dissembling you look for a true sign.
You search for a true word, for once not spoken in jest.
The diligent archer at first stands away from his target.
Tread softly, then, in your own house, in your own silence.

2

The wind shifts and heaves. Conversation this evening swings back and forth, beating sense vainly, an unlatched shutter. Our silence extends its red ribbon downward through rock, sinew, stone, quality, discourse, the floor of the world.

3

Fifty years on the road and the gate is within our grasp.
We may speak now of getting a grip or of coming to grips.
At the hexameter's end converge wisdom and apprehension.
Take hold with remembering hands; practise anapaest, spondee.

4

You raise the day slowly, an hour at a time. All its events
are the shaft that your presence of mind keeps in alignment.
Elsewhere the light flickers about the roof of old certainties.
You hold the day steady above your head with both hands.

5

Without longing, you draw history to the point of fable,
what's to come, to the point of venture without desire.
Being master of interval, you may occupy empty spaces,
in vacancy, strength and limit cultivate each new phrase.

6

Let us talk, as night falls, of integrity and deception,
of the way disappointments illuminate and hopes deceive.
At the crossover, spirit and form conjoin into substance
in this breath, all that is fabulous, all that is real.

7

We are the same now as silence and speech are the same,
or stillness and motion in this act wholly companioned.
Who can distinguish us from ourselves in this loosing?
Or tell us from what receives us, intimate as no other?

8

Thus it is to endure. Space, between action and action,
fills with regret, mirth, tears' residue or anticipation.
Let this moment, then, be the stillness of remainder.
In the next street, traffic stirs, crowds quicken the day.

Christopher Pilling

"Life Classes"

Since his translation of Tristan Corbière: *These Jaundiced Loves* (Peterloo Poets 1995), Christopher Pilling has published two collections of poems on paintings: *The Lobster Can Wait* (Shoestring 1998) and *In the Pink* (all on Matisse) and one on trees: *Tree Time* (both from Redbeck 1999 & 2003). His other writing has included two translations: a joint one with David Kennedy of Max Jacob – *The Dice Cup* (Atlas 2001) and one of Lucien Becker – *Love at the Full* (Flambard 2004); and two plays (the first with Colin Fleming) produced and performed by Keswick's Theatre by Lake: *The Ghosts of Greta Hall* (South Col Press 2001) and *Emperor on a Lady's Bicycle* (2001).

The life class oil paintings by 21 year old Kirsty Pilling – juxtaposed rather than directly linked with the poems – were exhibited at Thurrock College. She obtained a degree in Fine Art at Kent Institute of Art & Design, Canterbury, since when she has mainly undertaken private commissions, including the artwork for the covers of *Love at the Full*, and been a life-model herself.

OM (p.68) is a sacred syllable, usually intoned in Hindu devotion and contemplation.

Grateful thanks to the editor of *Brando's Hat* where *Midsummer Life Class* first appeared. And to Bridget, the midwinter model, to Sue, the midsummer model and to Alan Stones whose studio in Blencarn was where I wrote the first drafts. A classmate looking over was astonished: "This man's doing words!"

Christopher Pilling & Kirsty Pilling

MIDWINTER LIFE CLASS

I

A light rain on the roads at dawn has frozen
into glass — and to think I've chosen
to travel here by car by ice!

A light hand on the model's shoulder
would have slid as much — the light there, though, bolder
than any hand, is twice

as likely to keep its footing.
Her hair, with random strands jutting
into her profile, is, more's the pity,

almost solidly black but, with darting aubergine
glints on its disarray, the light is keen
to relish its ubiquity.

Now, in a changed position, she's rest-
ing on her left hand, her firm left breast
quite casually towards me — as is the *hauteur*

of her Roman nose — and the open tent
between taut rib-cage and arm is not meant
for sheltering from the light.

The groundsheet — cold, buff, nankeen
lined by shadows and far from pristine
— others having lain naked right

across it — is outshone by her more subtle flesh tones
that body me to her and make no bones
about being open to my sight,

which just as easily unfreezes, slipping over her.

II

The body's undulations end in a steep incline —
one leg perpendicular from the knee —
no chance of clambering up, no hold to put a foot in,
better take the path of least resistance, the fine line
between one buttock and the other, a gentle spin,
then ski gently
down the other leg — from hamstring to calf to shin.

III

Two members of the life class
saw the new pose as sexy.
(Just as the villagers predicted:
it all boils down to sex
and the exploitation of women.)

It can't be the mottled legs,
marbled with cold on the eve
of the winter solstice,
(The villagers had seen her coming,
happened to be at their window.)

I can't quite put my finger
on what it is, and there are some
who didn't think her sexy,
("It's not natural! We wouldn't
be seen dead, let alone...")

yet felt the sexiness in their
sketching, the lines taking over,
(... showing what not even
the menfolk could hope to see
on an ordinary winter's day.)

Full frontal, a prominent mole
on her midriff, goose pimples
round each nipple, black
pubic hair... ("Should be blacked out,
like windows in a war-zone.")

However warm the log stove
makes the studio ("No woman
should be subjected to such a
private thing!" a body bared
to an artist's wintry gaze),

she shivers, exercises her limbs:
they're quite natural, the
proportions we've given them,
and go on, when she's still again,
our pencils raised to confirm.

We admit the sensuous round
of belly, admit — and now a sneeze
takes everyone by surprise
and the model's suddenly here
in the flesh, convulsed in

her total mortal body (the one
the villagers discuss so freely
you'd think they had shares in her).
With the sneeze there's a pause,
strict pencils caught unawares.

IV

Now the model's faceless, a maelstrom of hair
swirling forward over a stool,
and the curves of her nape and shoulders stare
us into taking her as shapes
to be manipulated on paper with the untoward care
we might give to arranging drapes
over a body half-dead from hypothermia: a still
life, hair thrown over a stool, charged
with light's electricity, a cool
will
in a dead white flow of body, crying to be massaged.

V

Getting the model in position, with laughter
on all sides, charcoal at the ready,
not knowing what anyone else is after,
each has decided how they want her... "Steady,
everyone, if we must, we must compromise."
"Like this!" says one, curt
to the point of rudeness, showing
the posture he desires. "More to the right,
and lean a little," says another, growing
bold, baring her hurt
feelings, which up to then were tight
as breasts when the milk needs expressing.
The model starts undressing.
More views are directed at her.
"We needn't stifle
our artistic conception," says our leader,
temporising...
Unbidden,
the model's knee
comes up — she's settled the matter.
The other leg is hidden.
"Had an eyeful?"
A little taken aback, we *artists* doubt
now we'll ever be free
to draw her how we want. And don't we need a
certain composure...? No one should take a rise
out of us, not even the model.
But would we ever be found out
for giving her, let's say, two black thighs?

VI

My paper has guiding lines
but my writing is unguided.
It's linked by what's between
the raised knee of the model (who's chided
in jest for moving it when she sneezes),
and my eye which shines
now knee and eye are elided
in a thought which teases
me into meaning more than I thought I could mean.

VII

Déjeuner sur l'herbe
The Vegan model

We had lunch in the dining room.
Déjeuner, means the end of fasting.)
Bridget would eat no animal fat —
a Vegan who wouldn't cut the grass
thinking of the hurt to the blades...
Her lawn would be shoulder-high.

Back in the studio, we have lunch
again with Bridget naked on the grass.
There's hardly an ounce of fat on her.
I should have cut that line,
but we were chewing over the idea
of a naked woman hurt by grass blades.

We sit here fully clothed, full of ideas,
and an insatiable appetite
for Bridget's shoulder blades.

MIDSUMMER LIFE CLASS

I

A shoulder greets me as I enter,
a raised clavicle... Already I centre
on a part, but isn't that what we do —
our eyes immediately taken by a tattoo,
a strand of hair that's out of place,
as if there were an ideal, a state of grace
for any attribute, never mind the body whole?
You can only hear a cellist bow
a single note or chord at a time — you'll stitch
it gradually into a tune — for you to feel the itch
to get behind the notes, each run must sound
just right. Her feet are raised from the ground
on a dressed wooden block. One ankle
is damaged, a spot of blood won't rankle
for it forms a highlight in my painting.
To single it out avoids acquainting
myself with the grief of the harsh deed
which caused it. Grief, the word I need
for the overtone of Biblical sorrow,
is a sore on a line of verse, leave till tomorrow
any real emotion. Real emotion, I repeat
to let a little of it in, can be discreet,
but I can't see her as a sum of her parts
until her body expresses itself in heart to hearts
with me, and any feeling I have for her
must wait for the cello to become a blur
of one tune, her snuffle to be part of the cold
that will rack me and complete the mould.

II

To trace a line from toe to knee to hip
and then in a long convex sweep
to a pointed elbow is to delineate
a recumbent figure glad to let light
do the work for the class who's paying.
She can't stand us using her, spying
on her most intimate parts in the name
of art, she wants the money all the same.

The ring in her nose shouts "Fuck you!"
but she attempts to play down the blow
it can still cause those who don't know the form —
so pins and needles in her right arm
is only a bloody nuisance. She has to shake
it, but doesn't enough. Every prick's a prick
too many. She should have clenched her fists.
Might as well cure appetite with fasts.

III

If you sit around a naked body sketching
and reproduce its contours exactly
is it your sketch you most admire or the wretched
girl you've enjoyed quite matter of factly?

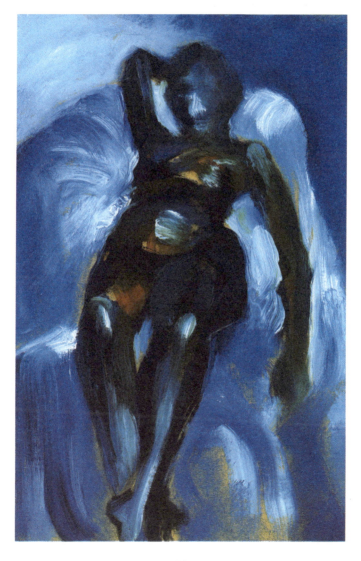

IV

W — a flying start. Plucked from the air.
W — the start of questioning.
Doubled-up — lying on her left hip.

In her shell. Her shell ear-ring
scintillates like sun on water.
Her stomach's a delta of stretch-marks

spelling M for mother.
She's running to mud on her soles.
She is the first letter of shell.

This way up, the tattoo is W
with Arabic extras. She'll tell me the word.
As an aside. An O word.

W on its side resembles a 3:
bare trunk on bare thigh on bare leg.
Bare arm makes an A if nose is the bar.

When do you adopt a posture like this?
Only if your world's at its end.
Already her feet are asleep.

W is the start of World. One world.
Wrench yourself back to life.

V

You are a landscape, a building, a still life.
No, you are none of these. Landscapes are not perturbed
by a random fly. Buildings stand expressionless.
Still lifes have a stillness you could never have,
however motionless you stand. The way you clasp
the top of that wooden chair, the way you centre
your gaze on a tangible beyond that must be
miles from any studio, the way you go there
and make the place your own, are how our eyes work.
We clasp you in lines and shading, woodenly maybe;
we see, or would wish to see, into and out with you
tangibly, giving you a beyond (what presumption!)
and that is where, with luck, we conjure you up,
a you out there, a whole body on paper here.

You've probably stripped us in your mind.
You're imagining our many blemishes and can find
more than we knew we had, ours and yours too.

VI

Tornadoes come closer with their cacophony
than you do, a thunder to your calm.
Their line of flight hellish monotony
for pilots; the folds across your midriff
more swirl and eventful for me —
your breasts. play hide them and seek them, your qualm
that these *artists* may make them flaccid, draw them skew-whiff
stiffening you. You'll damn well keep the folds tauter
than the lines constantly running
between the artists' fixed eyes
and your body — lines,
still alive life lines,
getting shorter
and shorter.

VII

The incommunicable sadness in your eyes
as you lie back and look up in a deckchair — no surprise
about that — but the upcurve
of your neck cannot help but emphasise
it without reserve.
The incommunicable sadness in your eyes
then distracts me from the rise
and fall of your breasts and the nerve
we have to expect you to epitomise
a sunbather and deserve
no respite from the drilling of our eyes.

The skylight sun started to shine on
you in this position and your jaded
mode; the stretched deckchair canvas looked fine on
your perimeter until, even as we watched, it faded.

VIII

Your breasts are not speaking to one another.
They face different ways, make their point
separately, but like many a sister and brother,
even ones who fall out when life is out of joint,
their areolas tell a similar story,
especially when they stand up for how they feel,
the left one humming OM, the right one the glory
of being human, fallen, outward-looking, real.

IX

Your left elbow is pointing at your navel.
Let it stay there and why not fall asleep?
Your legs are crossed and all ten toes
are making their points my way. Let them keep
their even temper and cross to us — bare feet
on a sunny beach and the sea flowing...
You yawn and close your eyes, don't see
the coastguard signal to the lifeboat going
off to rescue a girl out of her depth
in the whirls we've made of her — here
she can't touch bottom, there her left elbow
is a finger pointing out the pitfalls — all sheer.
Let's wake her — here's the fly to save
us the trouble. Come back to us from the deep.

John Weston

John Weston was born in 1938 and educated at Sherborne and Oxford where he read Greats. He spent 36 years in the Diplomatic Service, working in Asia, North America and continental Europe, and completed his career as Britain's Ambassador to the UN in New York. He now pursues a mixed portfolio of interests in education, the arts and the voluntary sector, also serving as a non-executive director on the boards of several companies including BT and Rolls-Royce. He is an Honorary Fellow of Worcester College Oxford; and is married with three children and one grandchild.

He began writing poems in 2002, many of them published in magazines. He won the Peterloo Open in 2004, and has a first collected volume due out from Peterloo in 2005.

For several poems here acknowledgements are due to: *The Spectator, The Interpreter's House, Scintilla, and The Shop*. 'Giving Way' won first prize in *Envoi Magazine*'s Competition in July 2003.

THE LAUNCH
(*For Marcus*)

I do not remember the house
where I was born, though the poem
(in my mother's voice) opened on
more than the sun's little window.

I must have grown ears like errant
wings at school when they recited
spells for how to gyre and gimble,
spread butter with the carpenter.

I tasted mellow fruitfulness;
saw silent flock in woolly fold;
wondered about his last duchess,
golden lamps, vegetable love,

and whether fifty springs sufficed
to stop winter icummen in.
I listened to Greek frogs croaking,
the ripple of Sabine fountain.

But you followed jumblies to sea
with 'sails as frail as autumn leaves',
leaving me standing in the lea
with 'less than one good line a day'.

It makes me think of my first bike –
the Coventry, and how they had
to push and push to get me to
take off; and the birdlike grace of

equilibrium finally
achieved, the blessing of surprise
at discovering that no hands
could mean flying even faster.

WINCHMORE HILL 1944

When I step from sunlight into cool
the sweetshop, serried jars like lungs,
wraps me in a breath
of sherbet and fresh tobacco.
My target for three ha'pence
after school in Vicars Moor Lane
lies there, in the humming frostbox.
The water-ice, tumbler shaped, is on a stick.
I'll have the one they call blackcurrant.
See how its crimson-purple syrop
sank to the bottom freezing.
Downside-up, once the first ice kiss
lets go my lips,
I'll suck that julep bruise straight out through the frost's pores.
From cave and magic carpet
I tramp home like a Bisto Boy,
the shop's zesty air still pricking my nostrils
sixty years on
(or was it peppermint?)

MY FATHER

He emerges from
the pages of his never-
to-be published verse
gesturing to me, as with
some forgotten semaphore –

'The Shrapnel Gleaners',
'Oak Trees', 'Afternoon Alert'.
So I too glean shards
from blitzed childhood memories,
rebuild his fractured presence,

matching his phrases
to precarious glimpses
over a lifetime,
and seeking now to summon
his ghost out of the shadows

for a belated
Festschrift. What coded sequence
has pushed my pen to
themes or images later
found prefigured in his own?

Broken health, broken
love – these poems I value
more now: lineaments
of a disappointed life,
but an honest monument.

It speaks still, the voice
comes and goes, as I read them,
eclipsing absence;
his own words like a handshake:
"How I pray he will not grieve".

OUT OF THE BLUE

email Bermuda: *"Are you by chance the JW*
for whose teddy-bear I once traded my camera,
at Elcot, near Kintbury, it must have been '48?
I still have the bear (called 'JW' from that date).
If I'm right, whatever became of the little box camera?
If mistaken, I really am sorry to trouble you."

Soon a careful hand-written letter arrives,
the teddy-bear's photo enclosed. My God, I remember!
My mother had given me him just after the War.
Still un-demobbed in khaki and scarlet, the bear
fixes me sternly, his eyes flashing jet and amber,
arms stretched in resignation. No Kodak survives.

'*Elcot*' – the shape of this word releases a flood:
childhood paradise of coppice and garden acres,
tall Wellingtonians with the spongy bark,
cock pheasants at ease among the boxed hedge-work,
nectarines fattening on the walled espaliers,
an abandoned orchard, a piggery beyond the wood

for hunting rats with an airgun, tame ferrets
in the converted hen-coop, my hidden 'residence'
up the copperbeech where I counted my secret hoard.
Hotel & Country Club said the painted board
after period fashion. The permanent residents
took tea from a silver urn. County friends would collect

later for cocktails and dinner ('Do try the jugged hare')
under a portrait rumoured to be by Gainsborough.
The radiogram 78s were Victor Silvester
and Edmundo Ros. Snooker or a round of canasta
crowned the extended evening. When finally through
'Nothing else like it for miles around' they'd declare.

It went bust of course. On the day for counting debts
my mother took off in her '39 Sunbeam, threatening
to kill herself. Hot in the wake to retrieve her
on Matchless 500 roared the official receiver
who stopped her in time. That same winter evening
I wept to be told we must go, leaving even the dogs.

The teddy-bear I suppose I must have outgrown,
or found was ill-matched to a boarding school address,
or perhaps never liked that much. The Brownie swap
(I'd thrown in an acrobat too) now sounds quite a snip:
is there more than a hint she gave it up under duress,
not quite trusting the words about parents' permission?

If so, no amount of diplomatic banter
can make amends to her now. Still, we're as one:
those random exchanges proved to hold a value
beyond the bargain under a Berkshire apple-tree,
like a child's balloon that has wafted across the ocean
and summons the past, and makes the world seem smaller.

SCILLIES IN APRIL

Running up to the Day-Mark
through spring heather
and high on the evening sea air,
I flushed the distant bird –
it launched on barred wings
sank fast within half a furlong
back into cover.

All the way back at full stretch
I searched my retina's sight-hoard
('look for the field-mark')
to earth the gaudy flash of
harlequin
with a sure connection;
my one recollection surely
too far outlandish.

Only after two days
did I catch Terry's mate on the
'Voyager of St Martin's',
to pep up his passengers, volunteering
"Have you heard, on Chapel Down
they've spotted a
hoopoe?"

O *upupa epops*! O song!
To have been on the mark all along!
Halloo small miracle, strange visitant,
shade of Aristophanes!
Last seen in April seven years ago
on a consular lawn
in Jerusalem.

EDWARDES SQUARE
(For My Daughter)

Not those spick Regency terraces
wrapped in wisteria nodosity,
but a 1940s corner block facing the pub
beside a world-ash.

A plinth in the hidden gardens
marks where the barrage balloon had
anchored through blitz, an errant galleon.
Half a century on

'Buster' too slipped her final moorings
from No. 14, sailed off with her promised
Bostonian key to Elysium, while we
scattered furtive ashes among the roses.

A boy, stripped to woollen bathing trunks,
I had swayed atop collapsible steps
to distemper ceiling and walls
in the minikin haven
that became her life's space.

Proudly I took there to tea
my first and last love.
The bells Auntie heard ring on –
she was so keen, she set
your mother and me back years.

In turn she dandled you awkward
watched by Peynet's porcelain lovers,
the swelling aquamarine roller
poised in its frame unbearably
to bear us all away.

Once, rusticated from boarding school,
we sent you to her in penance:
you said that loving confinement
was suffocating.

When she, blind and courageous, faltered,
you followed in, made it home.
New loves flared at the hearth:
such work and play as were hardly admitted
in 'Science and Health'.

Quitted now after two generations
this threshold recedes into history,
the bronzed deco doorknobs opening
only to memory.
But for each of you the shared gain,
with her blessing,
may yet sustain
a generation to come.

LAST RITES

That final day in Bedford hospital
the car-park man ticked me off, as I came out
'You can't leave yours there, you know'. 'I do know,'
I answered 'but your mother only dies once'.

She'd never adjusted to a life without work –
her bank of interests had too little left to draw on.
So in the small hours, when breathless anxiety struck,
comfort was slight, and I knew I was out of my depth.

'None of that sort of thing in *our* family' she insisted
when I rescued her from a psychiatric ward.
She was convinced they were secretly plotting against her,
which would have been funny except for her haunted eyes.

The end near, I was called to a different bedside.
She seemed more puzzled than frightened, even slightly indignant
when I ventured on her a passage from 'Revelation',
as if to say 'Not much of *that* in the family either'.

Her insistent 'Goodbye' at my whispered goodnight
before snatching sleep in an adjacent room
I realised only afterwards had meant what it said,
for with the dawn she sighed deeply, and stopped.

Her face suffused with a Lenten purple blush.
Kneeling I kissed her, drew the rings from her finger,
then rose to leave the orderlies to their business.
I felt she'd launched on Gerontius' great journey,

me on the nearer shore applauding her brave
life and her exit from it. In Ampthill churchyard,
'See, they return, and bring us with them' the stone said.
When at last I went back to clear her belongings,

as if possessed by a sudden mythic force
I fell on her bed, and felt bodying forth
a primal surge, an upwelling torrent of grief
sucking the breath out of me – a raw howl

the ear could hardly recognise as my own.
Knocking at the door, a neighbour below enquired
politely if a cup of tea might help, her gesture
the cue for all the familiars to reassemble.

TO ALASKA AND BACK

I knew I was losing you that day at Brooks Camp
where we walked to see the salmon leap
into the bears' open mouths
(they didn't even have to reach out).
Face to face with the big one on the return,
"Please bear, please bear ...." you intoned trembling,
and fragmenting before my eyes.
In the hotel, as I rang our Manhattan doctor,
you lay curled like an ancient foetus toward the wall.
Back on the East River, depression's gravity towed you
into an alien orbit, inert moon of a lost planet.
No more you to talk to about the 'you',
a film had descended between us,
mirror fogged as I lifted the morning razor.
Each day's pattern fractured in the making.
For months I scanned for lost wavelengths,
knew only skin-touch of severed limbs.
You had gone missing in front of me,
the companion who'd lurched from our tent
to die in the snow.
From the madness of Alaska's sunlit nights
to the city whose canyons offer no forgiveness,
time slowed toward the higher entropy, where
zero is a loop from the window.

The day you first noticed again the sky was blue,
I wept to remember the Kodiak bear,
and counted the evening stars, as they re-emerged.

A FAIR THOUGHT

Half way to oldfooldom no doubt,
I'd remarked on the statuesque
contours of the young singer from
the Guildhall School whose soprano
cadences in the Handel un-
hinged the ear, brimmed the eye with tears.

Later, talking of friends who had
parted, our tiff over pizza
was whether in ripe middle age
I could admire a beautiful
woman without lusting for her
(Fair do, whispered Mr. Hackett). *

Was I, you hazarded, giving
a cryptic clue to temptation
somewhere, somehow unresisted?
No. And on reflection I thought
it's like the innocent wonder
when wild trout display in mid-stream,

fallow deer dapple the foreground,
or that Kodiak bear stopped us:
the pulse quickens at such focus
through nature's bright lens. Even more
at this photo in my wallet –
your face, still young when we make love.

---

* "The lady now removing her tongue from the gentleman's mouth, he put his into hers. Fair do, said Mr Hackett".
Samuel Beckett, Watt 1953

HOUSE, AT DENBIGH GARDENS

Bricks-and-mortar craft,
buoyant in gravel eddies,
continental drift,
tacks for a new century,
hull down in the solar wind.

Inside, solid as
an Edwardian liner
and dressed overall,
it welcomes each boarding pair
with whisper of timber torque.

Anchored asylum
from 'earth filled with violence',
its constant bearing
has helped 'keep the seed alive',
hallow space for survival.

It survived bomb sticks
last time. The coloured glass panes
we restored to type;
from the garden's tidal depths
I still dredge shelter concrete.

One day we'll cast off
old moorings, when leaves lift at
intimations of bugles,
(the windows wink knowingly,
they have seen it all before) –

We shall look westward
over Mount Ararat Road,
seek that band of cloud
sailors know as Noah's Ark,
the wake stretching behind us.

GIVING WAY
("The Athabasca Glacier has retreated 1.5 kilometers since 1850")

The mountains rose to a spotless sky
that morning as we approached.
At the pass, moonscape:
in a valley bulldozed by behemoth forces,
acres of claggy moraine and rock.

Walking up over the debris we counted markers
signalling at decade intervals the farthest reach
of the glacier's toe, its secular melt-back.
In a few hundred yards we passed
my birth, my matriculation,
the flurry of children, our retirement.

We ventured on to the ice flow,
the air grew chiller, water chuckled unseen.
Striding ahead up the frozen slope
toward the grin of crevasses
I heard your anxious voice calling me back.

I turned, to recognise I must be standing
at my own graveside, the coming ebb point
where the glacier's mute recessional
would not mark time for me.

Together again going down, we observed
how alpine fireweed and parnassia
had already begun to repossess the abandoned marl.

As we left the icefield and drove on,
the weather changed.

TALISMAN

This Victorian penny,
bullet hole punched at the rim
where it winged the old Queen's crown,
has sat on my key-ring since

I filched it from *The White Hart's*
till, half a century back,
for luck. FID DEF's never let
me down, though the coin has worn

communion-wafer thin,
and in just one hundred years
the embossed flag has faded
from the shield of Britannia,

whose head (or what was left by
the wound exiting the oth-
-er side) is now floating in
a feuillemorte Valhalla cloud.

If I tilt it to the light,
the royal gaze is fixed, but
the lips move, the cheek allows
a faint porphyry blush. Touch,

it's my aged aunt's soft kiss
when she came in from the snow.
I pinch it between finger
and thumb, chafe the used metal.

ABOVE NORMAL

Implacable his gentle voice
down the line. My stomach tightens,
my words echo disembodied.

The wise course, expect further tests,
yes, he can recommend where next.
Your face is a Greek chorus mask.

Days, nights play in an altered key.
The Fates loom up from old pages:
sooner or later it's my lot.

The consultant gives a precise
percentage that there's a cancer:
this runner's no rank outsider.

Naked in blue hospital smock
I watch them go into the dark,
where with cracks like a staple gun

comes my turn to be invaded
and darts find their inner bulls-eye.
I dare not ask what X-rays show.

Six days to biopsy verdict.
You buoy me up with your life force;
mere man, I still cower at heart,

put off thinking tasks, fill hands by
sorting papers, polishing taps,
clean up the garden shed for spring –

banal count-down to what zero?
The comfort of cat's fur won't work,
my mind defaults to the worst case.

'You remember I told you there
is a one-in-seven chance you
have a tumour? The result's clear,

you are one   of the other six.'

Chastened, I wave shadows away.
They will return another day:
later not sooner, I still pray.

GRANDPARENTS

They hover like buddhas over our imaginings,
antique household gods who rode away on clouds
to make room for fresh devotions. Now occasional
visitors, leaning from framed sepia and damask
to enter the seasonal gathering at a happenstance, a phrase.

Down to earth in their day: the old man trying to salvage
a legacy's barren stake in Canadian uplands;
that grand dame, who mothered a tribe of seven
among them my father, making do in the blitzed city
and never revealing her answer to the infant's parroted question
("Granny, do *you* wear fully-fashioned bloomers?").

Entitled in turn, parents smiled on our
perpetuation of the name, as they moved from the effective
to the dignified in the family's constitution,
lavishing the little kindnesses, the hidden complicities;
and once in a while thrilling at their reach
over a generation, if a proud grandson should creep home
to show them a gasping trout hooked secretly
from the garden stream of a cordially disliked neighbour.

After their own translation, comes at length
the final act, when we lift to the news of our child's
approaching child already waving in the early scan,
and we must now busk the stage that filial piety requires,
until the last migration to that other Newfoundland where
grandparents have gone before us.

TO OUR FIRST GRANDCHILD, DAY ONE

Fat gold watch, indeed: perfect
miniature, your spring wound up
but three hours since, already
your hands tell us to count each
blessing, measure the future
by your forward direction.
Compact little half-hunter,
whose welcome chirrup signals
no alarm, whose face finds time
for life from moments of love.

SIGHTING

The night Mars passed closer in orbit
to us than it had for 60,000 years,
I took my grandson out to the huge sky
at the mature age of five weeks
to instruct him in the ways of the heavenly bodies.

His focus, let us admit, was at best blurred,
he had slight trouble keeping his concentration,
head lolling, eyes like shooting stars,
his cry was altogether more down to earth:
it was 2 a.m., and he'd lost the milky way.

I told him binoculars enhanced the red
and the bird-scope brought it out like a moon:
he was not impressed, but he made the point for me
that despite the galaxies' expanding dome
the greatest wonder of all was close at hand.

MOVING WITH **THE TIMES**

The clue for 20 across (7) reads
'How the past differs from the present'.
Ask Arthur Bryant & Malcolm Muggeridge,
whose Course on Democracy sounds intense.
Run a finger down the agony column:
note calls for unwanted artificial teeth;
£12 for Thucydides in mint condition;
for rheumatism, colonic irrigation.

I see a lady wishes to dispose
privately of her Rolls-Royce Phantom
and that her chauffeur's 'open for engagement'
(a garage with telephone is also free).
Perhaps she'll use the proceeds to acquire
the A.R.P. garden trench shelter –
a dozen dwarf Michaelmas daisies make
immense cushions, lilac, mauve or blue.

Next page the Lord Chancellor giving judgement
says the question is what does the word 'proportion' mean.
Revue's non-stop at the Windmill Piccadilly;
'*Wild Oats*' is playing at The Prince's.
Frost being less severe in the Vale of Evesham,
the asparagus crop has escaped damage.
In Saskatchewan drought-stricken farmers
send messages along their wire fences.

Obituaries mark the death of Schaliapin.
General Franco's troops have resumed
their advance to the sea. Allied experts
discuss the future size of battleships.
One hundred and forty-seven successive loops
have set a new record for a glider.
The RAF has vacancies for pilots.
Time-bomb explosion kills two in Haifa.

The ayes and noes have tied in the Commons.
The Member for Hexham said the motion only
added to Arab fears in Palestine:
The Speaker cast his vote for the Bill
extending citizenship there to migrants.
The Stock Market remains mostly steady.
I notice pure silk hailspot foulard is
used for a charming new frock from Debenhams.

Mothers are warned to keep babies from air
raid demonstrations. The pelts of Russian
dyed ermine make perfectly fitting boléros.
Conquer your nerves! Write for the free book!

My birth day puzzle makes no fitting sense
for who would understand the human state –
the clues today differ only in tense
from 13 April 1938.

FIFTY YEARS ON
(*For Sal*)

We still disagree about the exact moment:
whether the pews or the football terraces had it
and who spotted who first
in the smoky light of a Bristol afternoon.
Somehow we had fallen to walking together
and talking. I couldn't believe my luck at this turn
in what they'd arranged as a working weekend,
away from starched collars and straw boaters,
to see how the 'other half' lived in an urban parish,
courtesy of a fiery young priest called Mervyn.

The challenge in your glance seemed to signal,
beneath a hair-style borrowed from Dora Maar,
'Come on then, let's see what you're made of.'
Shyly exchanging addresses, I went back to school
hugging the biggest secret since the creation.
My early poems for you were in Latin couplets
because I hardly dared say it in English.
We both know now it was love at first sight
but for thirteen years I reckoned like a Ptolemy
before it dawned my orbit centred on you.

Random comings and goings replayed that journey
over Dartmoor to your sick-bed on my motorbike,
all skids and lost bearings under changing weather.
We each followed our own giddy diversions –
Nancy, Madrid, Dubrovnik; New York, and Hong Kong
where your delicate cast brought its fish to the rise:
at the end of your line to friends, that photograph
they casually played before me over the table
like a well presented mayfly – I took it away
and knew from that instant love could be a decision.

You stepped off the plane in your emerald coat,
and I saw this time it was real. Beneath two trees
in a Somerset lane you embraced me with your answer.
The day of our wedding I crossed the Avon Gorge
not even feeling Brunel under my feet
and still treading air when Bishop Mervyn pronounced
us man and wife in the same St Matthew Moorfields.
The de luxe dinner at Park's was £7.
Next morning we lifted off to China, joining
Li Po's journey of life, and 'sailing sunward'.

The Ming tower's armilla stood for our course
amid the din and garlic of the Peking air
and Red Guard madness raging like a Gobi dust-storm.
As the Embassy burned, the mob's blows only served
to temper your mettle. We lived and loved through it all
behind our moon-gate entrance in Sweet Rain Alley
or skating by floodlight on the Bei Hai
or hunting on bikes for a piece in yellow rosewood.
Leaving at last the blue-roofed Temple of Heaven,
did we imagine that echo of an unborn cry?

They came with a flurry, the children. I'd forgotton
how hard it was for you enacting the dutiful
mother and diplomat's wife; and how we had to
make our own beer, knead bread, and wait for the next
foreign post to recoup. From the surgeon's slab
to a career-on-the-rocks you never complained.
Our squalls blew themselves out, like Aprils of tears
washing an iris sky to the full prism
(no nimbus bruise on our horizons flagging
the late low troughs which nearly drowned us all).

Why did I always think of mandrake root
whenever we waved them off from another airport
or wrenched our life to a new peregrination,
kids growing taller in the surf, each parting
a small bereavement, which albums do not show
in the galloping carousel of summer holidays?

For you it was harder, the serial letting-go.
the vacant phases. Now, 'standing on their own feet'
they each return to us with handsome interest
your long investment of love from the beginning.

If life is opera, our curtain rose on Rossini –
the garrulous passion, the huge crescendi always
resolved in the major; then it was *Intermezzo*
or *Capriccio*, music and words interlaced
to weave from their filigrees of conversation
a sure intimacy that brought us through
all that epic folderol of public life
(the Don Magnificos, the betrayals and disguises)
to follow instead the whisper of our glade-boat
parting the diamond waters of the Okavango.

The kernel of our love now, is it this
constant surprise of gradualness, growing
like quilts or needlepoint, the Thonet chair's rattan
you peg in strip by strip, the indoor winter
seed-dibbling, the simmering brew of oranges
that cools in jars to prick the air with kumquat;
and our garden beyond, taking on the seasons,
where you bend to a shifting tapestry of greens,
faithful to your own Ithaca, as each spring
our magnolia chases night with a thousand candles?

That recent summer's day off Druidston,
Skomer on the skyline, waves on fire with light,
a camera caught us walking out of the sea,
hands linked, a spring in our step, as if
just baptised by Botticelli's Venus.
That's how I feel with you, still.
                            Backlit
by a couching sun, the snapshot stages us
kicking over our shadows' lengthening reach
while the little breakers behind shuffle us on,
and love's tide keeps flooding up the beach.

OTHER BOOKS FROM SHOESTRING PRESS

POEMS Manolis Anagnostakis. Translated into English by Philip Ramp. A wide ranging selection from a poet who is generally regarded as one of Greece's most important living poets and who in 1985 won the Greek State Prize for Poetry.
ISBN 1 899549 19 6   £8.95

HALF WAY TO MADRID: POEMS Nadine Brummer *Poetry Book Society Recommendation*.
ISBN 1 899549 70 6   £7.50

BROXTOWE BOY: A MEMOIR Derrick Buttress. ISBN 1 899549 98 6   £8.95

PASTORAL: POEMS Philip Callow. ISBN 1 904886 06 X   £8.95

TESTIMONIES: NEW AND SELECTED POEMS Philip Callow. With Introduction by Stanley Middleton. A generous selection which brings together work from all periods of the career of this acclaimed novelist, poet and biographer. ISBN 1 899549 44 7   £8.95

Shoestring Press also publish Philip Callow's novel, BLACK RAINBOW.
ISBN 1 899549 33 1   £6.99

TARO FAIR Ian Caws. ISBN 1 899549 80 3   £7.50

THE WEIGHT OF COWS Mandy Coe. ISBN 1 899549 97 8   £7.95

INSIDE OUTSIDE: NEW AND SELECTED POEMS Barry Cole. "A fine poet ... the real thing." *Stand*. ISBN 1 899549 11 0   £6.95

GHOSTS ARE PEOPLE TOO Barry Cole. ISBN 1 899549 93 5   £6.00

SELECTED POEMS Tassos Denegris. Translated into English by Philip Ramp. A generous selection of the work of a Greek poet with an international reputation.
ISBN 1 899549 45 9   £6.95

WHO Alan Dent.   ISBN 1 904886 07 8   £8.95

THE NEW GIRLS Sue Dymoke. ISBN 1 904886 00 0   £7.95

COLLECTED POEMS Ian Fletcher. With Introduction by Peter Porter. Fletcher's work is that of "a virtuoso", as Porter remarks, a poet in love with "the voluptuousness of language" who is also a master technician. ISBN 1 899549 22 6   £8.95

LAUGHTER FROM THE HIVE Kate Foley. ISBN 1 904886 01 9   £7.95

THE HOME KEY John Greening. ISBN 1 899549 92 7   £8.95

KAVITA TF Griffin. ISBN 1 899549 85 4   £6.50

LONG SHADOWS: POEMS 1957–2000 JC Hall. ISBN 1 899549 26 9   £8.95

A PLACE APART Stuart Henson. ISBN 1 899549 95 1   £7.95

CRAEFT: POEMS FROM THE ANGLO-SAXON Translated and with Introduction and notes by Graham Holderness. *Poetry Book Society Recommendation.*
ISBN 1 899549 67 6   £7.50

ODES Andreas Kalvos. Translated into English by George Dandoulakis. The first English version of the work of a poet who is in some respects the equal of his contemporary, Greece's national poet, Solomos. ISBN 1 899549 21 8   £9.95

OMM SETY John Greening. ISBN 1 899549 51 X   £5.95

FIRST DOG Nikos Kavvadias. Translated into English by Simon Darragh.
ISBN 1 899549 73 0   £7.95

A COLD SPELL Angela Leighton. *Other Poetry.* ISBN 1 899549 40 4   £6.95

WISING UP, DRESSING DOWN: POEMS Edward Mackinnon.
ISBN 1 899549 66 8   £6.95

ELSEWHERE Michael Murphy. ISBN 1 899549 87 0   £7.95

TOUCHING DOWN IN UTOPIA: POEMS Hubert Moore.
ISBN 1 899549 68 4   £6.95 Second Printing

MORRIS PAPERS: POEMS Arnold Rattenbury. Includes 5 colour illustrations of Morris's wallpaper designs. *Poetry Nation Review.* ISBN 1 899549 03 X   £4.95

MAKING SENSE Nigel Pickard. ISBN 1 899549 94 3   £6.00

THE ISLANDERS: POEMS Andrew Sant. ISBN 1 899549 72 2   £7.50

BEHIND THE LINES Vernon Scannell. ISBN 1 9004886 02 7 £8.95

MEDAL FOR MALAYA: a novel David Tipton. ISBN 1899549 75 7   £7.95

PARADISE OF EXILES: a novel David Tipton. ISBN 1899549 34 X   £6.99

STONELAND HARVEST: NEW AND SELECTED POEMS Dimitris Tsaloumas. This generous selection brings together poems from all periods of Tsaloumas's life and makes available for the first time to a UK readership the work of this major Greek-Australian poet.
ISBN 1 8995549 35 8   £8.00

AT THE EDGE OF LIGHT Lynne Wycherley. ISBN 1 899549 89 7   £7.95

TAKE FIVE: poems by Ann Atkinson, Michael Bartholomew-Biggs, Malcolm Carson, George Parfitt, and Deborah Tyler-Bennett. ISBN 1 899549 90 0   £7.95

For full catalogue write to:
Shoestring Press
19 Devonshire Avenue
Beeston, Nottingham, NG9 1BS UK
or visit us on www.shoestringpress.co.uk